BELIZE: HUMAN RIGHTS

EXECUTIVE SUMMARY

Belize is a constitutional parliamentary democracy. In March 2012 Prime Minister Dean Barrow's United Democratic Party (UDP) won 17 of the 31 seats in the House of Representatives following generally free and fair multi-party elections, albeit with some allegations of irregularities. Authorities failed at times to maintain effective control over the security forces. Security forces allegedly committed human rights abuses.

The most important human rights abuses included the use of excessive force by security forces, lengthy pretrial detention, and harassment and threats based on sexual orientation or gender identity.

Other human rights problems included domestic violence, discrimination against women, sexual abuse of children, trafficking in persons, and child labor.

In some cases the government took steps to prosecute officials who committed abuses, both administratively and through the courts, but successful prosecutions generally were limited in number and tended to involve less severe infractions. The prime minister disciplined two ministers for improper behavior, including removing one from a cabinet position. There was some impunity for high-ranking officials, but many lower ranking officials faced disciplinary action and/or criminal charges for alleged abuses.

Section 1. Respect for the Integrity of the Person, Including Freedom from:

a. Arbitrary or Unlawful Deprivation of Life

There were no reports that the government or its agents committed arbitrary or unlawful killings. Security force members occasionally used deadly force in the line of duty, and police officers were involved in three deaths of suspects in police custody. Authorities used police investigations, coroner's inquests, and the director of public prosecutions (DPP) to evaluate all killings by police.

Investigations continued into three deaths in police custody, in which police allegedly used deadly force under questionable circumstances.

On April 19, police shot and killed a man while responding to a burglary in progress. Police alleged the victim exited the home wielding a knife and crowbar and advanced toward the police before one officer shot him once in the abdomen. The victim's family, however, alleged that police shot him three times in the back while he was on the ground in police custody. As of October the case remained under criminal investigation.

b. Disappearance

There were no reports of politically motivated disappearances.

c. Torture and Other Cruel, Inhuman, or Degrading Treatment or Punishment

The constitution prohibits torture or other inhuman punishment, but there were reports that police used excessive force and other allegations of abuse by security force personnel.

The government occasionally ignored reports of abuses, withheld action until the case had faded from the public's attention, failed to take punitive action, or transferred accused officers to other areas within their department. The Ombudsman's Office stated it received numerous complaints of police abuse and that the public continued to fear the Gang Suppression Unit (GSU).

On May 27, an individual claimed that GSU officers entered his home and beat him. He said the officers told him that had he been alone, they would have killed him. The victim also alleged that, although GSU officers sought a warrant to search the house, they began the search before they got a warrant (see section 1.f).

According to the Ombudsman's Office, allegations of unlawful detention or abuse did not increase during the year following the government's November 2012 designation of five areas in Belize City as "crime ridden." In accordance with amendments to the Crime Control and Criminal Justice Act, this designation gave police expanded powers to execute searches, restrict movement in and out of the areas, and cordon off the areas (see section 1.f.).

There were widespread allegations of police refusing to respond to complaints and using excessive force. A tour guide required brain surgery after tourism police allegedly beat him in Caye Caulker in January. Police allegedly forced tourists who recorded the incident to destroy the footage. The police's internal investigation remained incomplete as of October.

Prison and Detention Center Conditions

Despite significant improvements over the last several years, prison conditions did not meet all international standards. A local nonprofit organization administered Belize Central Prison, the country's only prison, but the government retained oversight and monitoring responsibility. The government increased its oversight capability of the prison, adding two employees to the Comptroller of Prison's staff.

Physical Conditions: At the end of August, the prison held 1,650 inmates, including 47 women (plus one minor), 79 male juveniles, and 673 on remand. Prison capacity was approximately 1,750.

The regular prison population lived in cells accommodating approximately four to six persons. Prisoners on remand lived in a facility with approximately three to four persons per cell. Authorities also held some prisoners in the maximum-security section in the remand facility, usually with only one inmate per cell. Prison officials used isolation in a small, unlit, unventilated punishment cell, called a "reflection room," to discipline inmates in the youth section. Inmates had access to potable water.

Prison officials held women and men in separate facilities. The women's facility was located 200 yards outside the main compound. Conditions in the women's area were significantly better than in the men's compound. Officials housed female juveniles with the adult women.

Authorities held both on remand and convicted male juveniles separate from adult prisoners in two dormitories at the Wagner Youth Facility within the prison compound. Courts had convicted a quarter of the youth of major crimes, including murder, and many were gang members. Three minors escaped from the Wagner Youth Facility in August, and police recaptured two of them.

There were no reported cases of abuse or excessive force by prison officials, although prison officials noted that some prisoners were "roughed up" by police while in transit to the prison. Authorities recorded 93 inmate-on-inmate assaults by the end of August, including two instances where inmates were hospitalized with serious stab wounds. Prison officials noted that most assaults resulted from gang conflicts among the inmates, with more incidents happening in the remand population. There was one death due to complications related to HIV/AIDS and four due to other health concerns, including cancer, cirrhosis of the liver, and anemia. The prison had one full-time doctor, two nurses, and six emergency medical technicians to perform medical referrals to the Karl Heusner Memorial Hospital. Prison authorities hired a full-time psychologist, and a psychiatrist visited twice a month.

Administration: Prisoner recordkeeping was adequate. Various laws provide authorities the option to use alternative sentencing such as community service for nonviolent offenses, but there were no records for how often magistrates chose to use this option. Inmates had daily access to visitors, and the government did not restrict religious observance. A full-time chaplain coordinated visits by ministers from different denominations. The prison had a hall where church services took place. Prisoners could request other religious services, and the prison accommodated special dietary restrictions for prisoners whose faiths required them.

The law authorizes inmates to make complaints to the Ombudsman's Office through prison authorities, but inmates and their family members tended to submit such complaints directly to the ombudsman and did so without censorship. The Ombudsman's Office continued to follow up with prison authorities and visited with greater regularity than in previous years.

Independent Monitoring: Prison authorities permitted visits from independent human rights observers, including representatives from the diplomatic community and international and local nongovernmental organizations (NGOs).

Improvements: After assuming responsibility for prison operations in 2002, the Kolbe Foundation made significant improvements during the year in security as well as conditions for inmates, including the establishment of rehabilitation and education centers, and it initiated programs to reduce inmate-on-inmate violence, provide HIV/AIDS services, and provide medical care. Kolbe also overhauled training to improve security, address proper treatment of inmates, and minimize petty corruption.

The Labor Commissioner released a formal report after receiving complaints about employment irregularities from some employees and ex-employees of the Kolbe Foundation. As a result of the report, the Kolbe Foundation formalized their disciplinary procedures and hired a new chief of security to investigate officers and incidents and an intelligence officer to seek out irregularities amongst the guards.

During the year the prison operator continued to increase staff training, installed a potable water system, installed security scanners, installed a public address system for educational purposes, formalized its Quick Response Team, and made additional progress separating members of rival gangs.

d. Arbitrary Arrest or Detention

Although the constitution and law prohibit arbitrary arrest and detention, there were occasional allegations that the government failed to observe these prohibitions. Due to substantial delays and a backlog of cases in the justice system, in some cases courts did not try minors until they turned 18, although charges proceeded based on the age of the suspect when the crime was committed.

Role of the Police and Security Apparatus

The Ministry of National Security supervises the Belize Defense Force (BDF) as well as the Belize Coast Guard and the Belize Police Department (BPD). Although primarily charged with external security, the BDF also provides domestic security support to civilian authorities. BDF soldiers frequently worked alongside police officers, particularly in Belize City. BDF personnel assisting police have limited powers of arrest; police take the lead when making arrests. Low pay for security officers and corruption remained problems. There were several cases of alleged abuse by the police.

The Professional Standards Branch (PSB) is charged with investigating complaints against police. An assistant commissioner of police headed the PSB, supported by seven officers. One inspector and two special constables covered the entire country except for the Belize District, and one assistant superintendent, one sergeant, and two corporals covered Belize City and District. The law authorizes the police commissioner to place police personnel on suspension or interdiction (which is suspension, potentially with garnished wages). The PSB received 120 formal complaints of alleged police misconduct as of September. The government provided no information regarding the number of officers placed on interdiction or whether it sought criminal charges or disciplinary action in any of the cases.

The PSB continued to receive complaints against the BPD's GSU. The media reported several incidents of police using excessive force, including at least two involving the GSU.

Arrest Procedures and Treatment of Detainees

Police must obtain search or arrest warrants issued by a magistrate, except in cases of hot pursuit, when there is probable cause, or when the presence of a firearm is suspected, or cases covered by the new Crime Control and Criminal Justice Act. The government amended and expanded the law in February to allow for unlimited areas to be labeled "crime ridden areas" (see section 1.f.). Generally police must inform a detainee of his rights at the time of arrest and of the cause of his detention within 48 hours of arrest. Police must also bring a detainee before a magistrate to be charged officially within a reasonable time (no more than 48 hours). The BPD faced allegations that its members arbitrarily detained persons, did not take detainees to a police station in the required manner, and used detention as a means of intimidation.

The law requires police to follow the Judges' Rules, a code of conduct governing police interaction with arrested persons. Although judges sometimes dismissed cases that involved violations of the Judges' Rules, they more commonly deemed confessions obtained through violation of these rules to be invalid. Police usually granted detainees timely access to family members and lawyers, although there were occasional complaints that authorities denied inmates access or a telephone call after arrest.

Persons charged with minor offenses are eligible for bail, but persons charged with more serious crimes, including murder, gang activity, possession of an unlicensed firearm, and specified drug trafficking or sexual offenses, must apply to the Supreme Court for bail.

Pretrial Detention: Case backlogs in the docket often caused considerable delays and postponement of hearings, occasionally resulting in prolonged pretrial detention. The time lag between arrests, trials, and convictions ranged from six months to four years and occasionally longer. Pretrial detention for persons accused of murder averaged three to four years.

e. Denial of Fair Public Trial

The constitution provides for an independent judiciary, and the government generally respected judicial independence. Persons have the right to bring legal actions for alleged violations of rights protected under the constitution, regardless of whether there is also implementing legislation.

Trial Procedures

The law provides for all citizens the right to a fair trial, and an independent judiciary generally enforced these rights. A magistrate generally issues decisions and judgments for lesser crimes after deliberating on the arguments presented by the prosecution and defense.

Legislation passed in 2011 stipulates that nonjury trials be mandatory in cases involving murder, attempted murder, abetment of murder, and conspiracy to commit murder. A single Supreme Court judge hears these cases. This legislation passed despite public opposition by individuals, legal practitioners, and human rights activists. During the year juries heard the majority of tried cases dated before the law's passage.

Defendants enjoy a presumption of innocence and have the right to defense by counsel, a public trial, and appeal. The court has the authority to exclude defendants from the courtroom if it determines that the opposing party has a substantiated fear for his/her safety, in which case the court can grant interim provisions that both parties be addressed individually.

A Legal Aid and Advice Center, staffed by three attorneys, can provide legal services and representation for a range of civil and criminal cases, including cases of domestic violence and criminal cases up to attempted murder. There is no requirement for defendants to have legal representation except in cases involving murder. The Supreme Court's registrar has the responsibility of appointing an attorney to act on behalf of indigent defendants charged with murder. In lesser cases the court does not provide defendants an attorney, and defendants sometimes represent themselves rather than hire an attorney. Defendants are entitled to adequate time and facilities to prepare a defense or to request an adjournment, often used by the defense as a delaying tactic. Defendants may not be compelled to testify against themselves or confess guilt. Defendants have the right to appeal their sentences to a higher court.

The law allows defendants to confront and question witnesses against them and to present witnesses on their behalf, but a 2010 law allows written statements by witnesses to be admitted into evidence in place of court appearances. Judges generally admitted a statement if it was complemented by other evidence pointing to the defendant's guilt, but were sometimes reluctant to admit witness statements without the presence of the witness at the trial if it was the sole or main evidence suggesting guilt. A 2012 law allows the prosecution to submit the content of previous testimony as official statements when the witness was a hostile witness, rather than allowing the statement to be used only as proof that the witness provided different testimony earlier. Judges remained reluctant, however, to allow the prosecution to submit into evidence previous testimony as official statements in instances of hostile witnesses, and judges and juries were less likely to convict solely on statements. The Office of the Director of Public Prosecutions reported a conviction rate of 25 percent for cases that proceeded to prosecution. Defendants have the right to produce evidence in their defense and examine evidence held by the opposing party or the court.

Lengthy trial backlogs remained, particularly for serious offenses such as murder. The DPP stated that, as of September more than 100 murder cases awaited trial. Problems included police delays in completing their investigations, court delays in preparing depositions, and adjournments in the courts. Judges occasionally were slow to issue rulings, taking a year or longer. The rate of acquittals and cases withdrawn by the prosecution due to insufficient evidence continued to be high, particularly for murder and gang-related cases, often due to failure of witnesses to testify because of fear for life and personal safety. Several witnesses were killed in earlier years. In February police recovered the body of a witness to a 2006 murder who had been missing for more than two months after leaving protective custody. Authorities suspected foul play and an investigation was under way.

Political Prisoners and Detainees

There were no reports of political prisoners or detainees.

Civil Judicial Procedures and Remedies

Citizens may seek civil remedies for human rights violations. The Supreme Court hears most civil suits, but the magistrates' courts have jurisdiction over civil cases involving sums of less than 5,000 Belize (BZ) dollars ($2,500). In addition to civil cases, the Supreme Court has jurisdiction over cases involving human rights issues. The backlog of civil cases in the Supreme Court was significant and increased during the year. During the year the Supreme Court, in partnership with the University of the West Indies (Belize), launched a mediation program to address the rising backlog of civil cases. The program trained the first cohort of 50 mediators in the summer.

Litigants may appeal their cases to the Caribbean Court of Justice, the country's highest appellate court.

f. Arbitrary Interference with Privacy, Family, Home, or Correspondence

The constitution prohibits such actions, and government authorities generally respected these prohibitions.

In November 2012, however, the government invoked an existing, but previously unused, law that allows the government to declare one-square-mile zones "crime ridden areas" where security officers have the authority to search buildings and individuals without obtaining search warrants or stating a cause. Police searched more than 200 persons before the searches were approved by the mostly inactive Crime Control Council and published in the official *Gazette*, both of which the law requires. In December 2012 authorities expanded the law to cover an indefinite area, moved the approval requirement to the National Security Council from the more independent Crime Control Council, and expanded the length of time an area could be labeled as crime ridden. The government implemented the law through January. Citizens complained in the media about excessive force used by police during those searches, but the ombudsman's office reported no increase in complaints during this time.

Law enforcement agencies may, with judicial oversight, intercept communications to obtain information in the interest of "national security, public order, public morals, and public safety." The law defines communication broadly to encompass the possible interception of communication by post, telephone, facsimile, e-mail, chat, or text messages whether encrypted or unencrypted and whether via public or private providers.

Section 2. Respect for Civil Liberties, Including:

a. Freedom of Speech and Press

The law provides for freedom of speech and press, and the government generally respected these rights. An independent press, an effective judicial system, and a functioning democratic political system combined to promote freedom of speech and press.

Internet Freedom

There were few government restrictions on access to the internet and no credible reports that the government monitored e-mail or internet chat rooms without appropriate legal authority. The World Bank estimated that 25 percent of the population had access to the internet.

Academic Freedom and Cultural Events

There were no government restrictions on academic freedom or cultural events.

b. Freedom of Peaceful Assembly and Association

The law provides for freedom of assembly and association, and the government generally respected these rights, with the exception of areas determined to be crime ridden (see section 1.f.).

c. Freedom of Religion

See the Department of State's *International Religious Freedom Report* at www.state.gov/j/drl/irf/rpt.

d. Freedom of Movement, Internally Displaced Persons, Protection of Refugees, and Stateless Persons

The constitution provides for freedom of internal movement, foreign travel, emigration, and repatriation, and the government generally respected these rights. The government cooperated with the Office of the UN High Commissioner for Refugees (UNHCR) and other humanitarian organizations in providing protection and assistance to internally displaced persons, refugees, returning refugees, asylum seekers, stateless persons, and other persons of concern.

Protection of Refugees

Access to Asylum: The laws provide for the granting of asylum or refugee status, but the government has not established a system for providing protection to refugees. The NGO Help for Progress, the UNHCR's implementing partner in the country, assisted with refugee and asylum cases. The Immigration and Nationality Department handles individual cases but has not issued refugee permits in almost 15 years.

The Immigration Department worked with Help for Progress to determine the eligibility of persons claiming refugee status or asylum. The department established an Eligibility Committee for Refugee Status Determination, but it did not meet. The NGO continued to report an increase in asylum seekers who claimed to be victims of, or threatened by, gangs and organized crime, primarily from El Salvador and Guatemala. Help for Progress also operated a government-subsidized shelter for asylum applicants and refugees. The Immigration Department generally offered renewable special residency permits for periods of 60 to 90 days to asylum seekers with the possibility of permanent residency and citizenship after extensive stays.

Section 3. Respect for Political Rights: The Right of Citizens to Change Their Government

The constitution provides citizens the right to change their government peacefully, and citizens exercised this right through periodic, generally free and fair elections held by secret ballot and based on universal suffrage for all citizens age 18 and older.

Elections and Political Participation

Recent Elections: In March 2012 the UDP won 17 of 31 seats in the House of Representatives, giving it a parliamentary majority in generally free and fair elections, with some allegations of irregularities. The opposition People's United Party (PUP) challenged the results in three constituencies, while the UDP challenged one constituency won by the opposition. The Supreme Court upheld the election results in all four constituencies. For the first time, an Organization of American States team officially monitored elections, calling them "clean and efficient."

Participation of Women and Minorities: There were five women in the 13-member appointed Senate and one woman in the 31-seat elected House of Representatives. Mestizo, Creole, Maya, Garifuna, Mennonite, and other minority and immigrant groups participated in the National Assembly and at high levels of government. There were two female ministers in the 21-member cabinet.

Section 4. Corruption and Lack of Transparency in Government

The law provides criminal penalties for corruption by officials, but the government did not implement the law effectively, and officials sometimes engaged in corrupt practices. The World Bank's worldwide governance indicators reflected that corruption continued to be a problem.

Corruption: Following years of widespread allegations of corruption within the Department of Immigration, in February the minister of immigration made changes to tighten passport procedures and increase accountability. In September the prime minister expelled Minister of State Elwin Penner from the cabinet after an investigation uncovered allegations that he illegally assisted a non-Belizean citizen to obtain Belizean citizenship and receive a Belizean passport. Authorities also suspended one high-level Department of Immigration official and two lower-level officials, pending the results of the investigation. This discovery followed the implementation of new, stricter passport regulations. As of October the investigation continued.

The government also held other high-level officials accountable for their behavior. Minister of State Mark King was suspended for three months from the cabinet without pay after allegedly punching a police officer and brawling in public while intoxicated. Authorities cleared King of the charges in mid-June.

For the first time, the government convened the Public Accounts Committee (PAC) to evaluate and make recommendations on the auditor general's reports on public spending. Although by law a bipartisan committee, the two opposition PUP members (including the chair) boycotted the PAC's meetings, contending the majority UDP members were improperly handling the issue.

The Office of the Ombudsman has authorization to investigate allegations of corruption as well as other complaints. Individual agencies use various internal methods to investigate misconduct by their officials. For example, the Department of Immigration and Nationality investigated complaints on an ad hoc basis. Additionally, the Office of the Auditor General is empowered to ensure government accountability of public finances. That office produces an annual report and – when called upon – special audits into government spending. It has the authority to access financial records and highlight irregularities. The ombudsman and the auditor general did not collaborate with civil society, because such organizations rarely engaged on the issue of corruption.

Whistleblower Protection: No laws provide protection to public and private employees for making internal disclosures or lawful public disclosures of evidence of illegality.

Financial Disclosure: The Prevention of Corruption in Public Life Act requires public officials to submit annual financial disclosure statements, which the Integrity Commission reviews. At the same time, the constitution allows authorities to prohibit citizens from questioning the validity of such statements. Anyone who questions these statements orally or in writing, outside a rigidly prescribed procedure, is subject to a fine of up to BZ$5,000 ($2,500), imprisonment of up to three years, or both. There were no reports that authorities invoked this prohibition during the year. The body governing financial disclosure did not function, and no financial disclosure statements were submitted.

Public Access to Information: The law provides for public access to documents of a ministry or prescribed authority upon written request, although it protects a number of categories, such as documents from the courts or those related to national security, defense, or foreign relations. The government must supply to the office of the ombudsman a written reason for any denial of access, the name of the person making the decision, and information on the right to appeal. There was no public outreach or training relating to public access to information during the year.

Section 5. Governmental Attitude Regarding International and Nongovernmental Investigation of Alleged Violations of Human Rights

A variety of domestic human rights groups generally operated without government restriction, investigating and publishing their findings on human rights cases. Government officials often were cooperative and responsive to their views.

Government Human Rights Bodies: The ombudsman, although appointed by the government, acts as an independent check on governmental abuses. A new ombudsman started his three-year term in January after the position had been vacant since December 2011. The new ombudsman hired a lawyer to assist with legal questions and investigations. The ombudsman's office holds a range of procedural and investigative powers, including the right to enter any premise to gather documentation and the right to summon persons. The office operated under significant staffing and financial constraints. The law requires the ombudsman to submit annual reports, and the office presented the report for 2012 to the government cabinet. The office also created a mid-year report to address problem trends, which was encouraged by the cabinet.

The ombudsman's office reported continuing difficulties receiving information from the BPD regarding allegations made against the BPD.

The Human Rights Commission, an independent, volunteer-based government agency, continued to operate, but only on an ad hoc basis, constrained by funding and staffing limitations. NGOs and other organizations noted that the Human Rights Commission was more active and vocal than in previous years.

Section 6. Discrimination, Societal Abuses, and Trafficking in Persons

The constitution prohibits discrimination based on race, gender, disability, language, or social status, and the government generally enforced these prohibitions.

Women

Rape and Domestic Violence: The criminal code criminalizes rape, including spousal rape. The code states that a person convicted of rape or marital rape shall be sentenced to imprisonment of eight years to life, although in practice sentences were sometimes much lighter. Generally, challenges to the wider justice system resulted in poor conviction rates for rape offenses. A number of cases resulted in acquittals or discontinuance because the accusing party dropped the charges or refused to testify at trial. In many instances the failure to proceed with a case was caused by the victim's fear for personal safety. The BPD reported 28 cases of rape and 13 arrests in 2012. Underreporting of rape was likely due to perceived inefficiencies in the police and judicial systems as well as fear of further violence, retribution, and social stigma. Reports and charges laid for "carnal knowledge," commonly known as "statutory rape" in other contexts, increased dramatically. At the end of August, police noted reports of carnal knowledge increased 51 percent over the previous year. Anecdotal evidence suggested this was not a reflection of more crimes being committed but rather an indication of increased reporting, likely due to better public education on the issue and the protection of minors' names by the National Council for Families and Children.

Domestic violence is frequently prosecuted with charges such as "harm," "wounding," "grievous harm," rape, and marital rape. Police, prosecutors, and judges recognize both physical violence and mental injury. Penalties include fines or imprisonment for violations; the level of fine or length of sentence depends on the crime. The law empowers the Family Court to issue protection orders against accused offenders. Persons who may apply for protection orders against domestic violence include de facto spouses or persons in visiting relations. Protection orders may remain in place for up to three years and may include a requirement for child maintenance (support) where applicable.

The Women's Department under the Ministry of Human Development and Social Transformation continued its campaign against gender-based and domestic violence. The department used several handbooks, including women's rights, sexual violence, and domestic violence handbooks, for training and sensitization, and a sexual violence protocol that served to guide responses by key agencies, including the police and the Department of Human Services in reporting and providing care to victims. The Women's Department conducted several public awareness presentations and sensitization trainings throughout the year. The department also continued its intervention and prevention program for men who were abusive to women. It received referrals from both the criminal and civil courts. The BPD continued to operate a toll-free domestic violence hotline.

Despite these efforts, domestic violence against women remained a significant problem; information regarding the number of cases during the year was not available. Domestic violence was most prevalent in the Belize District, which includes Belize City. There were two women's shelters in the country (with a total of 18 beds) that offered short-term housing. There were no transitional or medium-term shelters to assist victims to move toward independent living.

Sexual Harassment: The law provides protection from sexual harassment in the workplace, including provisions against unfair dismissal of a victim of sexual harassment in the workplace. The Women's Department recognizes sexual harassment as a subset of sexual violence.

Reproductive Rights: Couples and individuals have the right to decide freely and responsibly the number, spacing, and timing of their children; the UN Fund for Population reported that the maternal mortality rate was less than 50 per 100,000 live births. Programs undertaken by the Ministry of Health and the Belize Family Life Association provided information and access to family planning and reproductive health services; skilled personnel attended 95 percent of births.

Discrimination: Despite legal provisions for gender equality, NGOs and other observers believed that women faced social and economic discrimination. The law mandates equal pay for equal work. The government had programs aimed at empowering women. The law provides generally for the continuity of employment and protection against unfair dismissal, including for sexual harassment in the work place, pregnancy, or HIV status. It also addresses procedures for the termination of contract and establishes a labor complaints tribunal.

In May the government launched its Revised National Gender Policy (RNGP), a comprehensive, government-wide strategy to promote gender equality.

The Women's Department is responsible for programs to improve the status of women. A number of NGOs focused on women's issues also worked closely with various government ministries to promote social awareness programs relating to gender equality.

There were no legal impediments to women owning or managing land or other real property. Despite participating in all spheres of national life, women held relatively few top managerial positions. The labor commissioner verified that men traditionally earn more because they hold higher managerial positions. Women outnumbered men in university classrooms and in high school graduation rates. The law mandates equal pay for equal work and was generally respected. The labor commissioner received no complaints by women relating to unequal pay. According to a 2012 government survey, women accounted for 40 percent of the labor force and experienced higher rates of unemployment – 22 percent compared with 9 percent for men. The same survey noted that 52 percent of women participated in the labor force, in comparison with 79 percent of men.

Children

Birth Registration: Citizenship is derived by birth within the country's territory, regardless of the nationality of the parents. Citizenship may also be acquired by descent if at least one parent is a citizen of the country, but citizenship by descent is not automatic for a child born outside the country. The law requires the registration of the birth of children within 42 days of birth. During the year the UN Children's Fund, working in partnership with government agencies, completed universal birth registration, two years in advance of the 2015 deadline.

Child Abuse: No data was available regarding the number of cases of domestic violence and of sexual abuse against children under 14 reported during the year. In 2011 there were 159 cases of domestic violence against children under age 14 and 63 cases of sexual abuse against children under age 14.

The law allows authorities to remove a child from an abusive home environment and requires parents to maintain and support children until the age of 18.

There were publicized cases of underage young women being victims of sexual abuse and misconduct, in some instances after persons known to them solicited them online.

The Family Services Division in the Ministry of Human Development and Social Transformation is the government office with the lead responsibility for children's issues. The division coordinated programs for children who were victims of domestic violence, advocated remedies in specific cases before the Family Court, conducted public education campaigns, investigated cases of trafficking in children, and worked with local and international NGOs and UNICEF to promote children's welfare.

Forced and Early Marriage: The legal minimum age to marry is 18, but persons between ages 16 and 18 can marry with the consent of parents, legal guardians, or judicial authority. According to the 2011 Multiple Indicator Cluster Survey, 15 percent of women between the ages of 15 and 19 were married.

Sexual Exploitation of Children: In February the government passed new laws increasing criminal penalties and improving protections for victims of trafficking and of the criminal sexual exploitation of children. The Criminal Sexual Exploitation of Children Act introduces penalties related to child prostitution, child pornography, child sexual exploitation, and indecent exhibition of a child. This law also permits 16- and 17-year-old children to engage in sexual activity in exchange for remuneration, gifts, goods, food, or other benefits. NGOs expressed concern that this specific clause in the law could render children vulnerable to commercial sexual exploitation given the common practice of parents' pushing their children to provide sexual favors to older men in exchange for remuneration. The legal age for consensual sex is 16. "Carnal knowledge" of a girl under the age of 14, with or without her consent, is an offense punishable by 12 years' to life imprisonment. Carnal knowledge of a girl 14-16 years of age is an offense punishable by five to 10 years' imprisonment. The prime minister's wife, who is the country's special envoy for women and children, publicly advocated against the sexual exploitation of children.

There were anecdotal reports that boys and girls were involved in child prostitution, including the so-called "sugar daddy" syndrome where older men provided money to young women and/or their families for sexual relations, as well as possible sex tourism. The law criminalizes the procurement or attempted procurement of unlawful carnal knowledge with a female who is under the age of 18 and who is not a person engaged in prostitution or of "known immoral character"; an offender is liable to five years' imprisonment. Sex with anyone age 16 or under is a criminal offense.

The criminal code establishes a penalty of two years' imprisonment for persons convicted of publishing or offering for sale any obscene book, writing, or representation.

International Child Abductions: The country is a party to the 1980 Hague Convention on the Civil Aspects of International Child Abduction. For information see the Department of State's report on country-specific information at http://travel.state.gov/abduction/country/country_3781.html.

Anti-Semitism

There were no reports of anti-Semitic acts. There were fewer than 10 members in the Jewish community.

Trafficking in Persons

See the Department of State's *Trafficking in Persons Report* at www.state.gov/j/tip.

Persons with Disabilities

The law does not expressly prohibit discrimination against persons with physical, sensory, intellectual, and mental disabilities in employment, education, air or other transportation, access to health care, or the provision of other state services. The constitution provides for the protection of all citizens from any type of discrimination. The law does not provide for accessibility to persons with disabilities and most public and private buildings and transportation were not accessible to them. There were no policies to encourage hiring of persons with disabilities in the private or public sectors.

Informal government-organized committees for persons with disabilities were tasked with public education and advocating for protections against discrimination. Private companies and NGOs provided services to persons with disabilities. The Ministry of Education maintained an educational unit offering limited special education programs within the regular school system. There were two schools and four special education centers for children with disabilities.

The special envoy for women and children continued advocacy campaigns on behalf of persons with disabilities and supported the NGO CARE-Belize effort to promote schools that made efforts to create inclusive environments for persons with disabilities. She continued to raise funds for an Inspiration Center to offer basic medical care and therapies for children with special needs, as well as assistance for at-risk youth. In August UNICEF and local partners launched the Situational Analysis of Children with Disabilities and the Situational Analysis of Blind and Visually Impaired Children. The analysis showed that 36 percent of children between the ages of two and nine were at risk of having one or more disabilities, whether physical, auditory, visual or a learning disability. This represented a 10 percent increase since 2006.

Indigenous People

No separate legal system or laws cover indigenous persons, since the government maintains that it treats all citizens the same. Employers, public and private, generally treated indigenous people equally with other ethnic groups for employment and other purposes.

Among the country's indigenous population, the Mopan and Q'eche have historically been referred to under the general term Maya, although self-proclaimed leaders more recently asserted that they should be identified as the Masenal (common people). The Maya Leaders' Alliance, which comprised the Toledo Maya Council, Q'eche Council of Belize, Toledo Alcaldes Association, the Julian Cho Society, and the Tumul K'in Center of Learning, monitored development in the Toledo District with the goal of protecting Maya land and culture. According to a representative of the Maya Leaders Alliance, the government, without consulting the Maya community, renewed petroleum exploration concessions that included territories over which the Supreme Court gave the Maya community some jurisdiction in a 2010 decision.

The legal dispute over the land rights of the Maya continued during the year. The 2010 Supreme Court decision and a subsequent Court of Appeals decision in July stated that the Maya community had certain authorities over some lands in the Toledo District. The July decision, however, reversed the requirement that the government develop implementation mechanisms. Both sides appealed the Court of Appeals' ruling to the Caribbean Court of Justice. The Sarstoon Temash Institute of Indigenous Management (SATIIM) filed a second court case against the government and the oil concessionaire to determine if the Sarstoon Temash National Park was indigenous or government-owned land and if the oil company had the right to explore and drill within the park's boundaries. The original Maya lands case proceeded to the Caribbean Court of Justice in November while a decision remained pending for SATIIM.

Societal Abuses, Discrimination, and Acts of Violence Based on Sexual Orientation and Gender Identity

The criminal code states that "carnal intercourse" with any person "against the order of nature" shall receive a punishment of 10 years' imprisonment. This law was interpreted as including only sex between men. Additionally, the Immigration Act prohibits "homosexual" persons from entering the country, but immigration authorities did not enforce that law.

In May the National Women's Commission launched its Revised National Gender Policy (RNGP), which, along with other language on gender equality, added sexual orientation as a protected status.

The legal challenge by a member of the NGO United Belize Advocacy Movement's (UniBAM) against the "carnal intercourse" law continued during the year. In July the court heard substantive arguments, but the court's decision on the constitutionality of the law had not been handed down as of November.

A Jamaican LGBT rights activist based in Canada filed a case challenging the immigration law with the Caribbean Court of Justice. The hearing began in mid-November.

The extent of discrimination based on sexual orientation or gender identity was difficult to ascertain due to lack of reporting instances of discrimination through official channels. Local LGBT rights advocates noted that LGBT persons feared the police and had been harassed while reporting unrelated crimes.

UniBAM, the country's first legally registered LGBT advocacy organization, reported that continuing harassment and insults by the public affected its activities, and its members were reluctant to file complaints. The UniBAM director reported multiple physical attacks and harassment of members of UniBAM's board of directors and other members of the LGBT community and their family members. Several members of the LGBT community reported receiving death threats.

There were marches against the sexual orientation portion of the RNGP throughout the country, often with hundreds of citizens participating. One march featured a figure hanging from a noose with the name "UniBAM" inscribed on its chest. One gay-friendly protest was organized during the year, in response to opposition to the RNGP. Organizers rescheduled a transgender fashion show due to concerns over the public's possible adverse reaction. In the context of the public controversy over the RNGP, the prime minister and his wife separately gave public remarks in support of equal rights for all, the first time such remarks were made by high-level public officials.

Two other organizations completed the process of filing legal papers to become recognized NGOs working on advocacy group for lesbian and bisexual women and LGBT youth.

Other Societal Violence or Discrimination

There was some societal discrimination against persons with HIV/AIDS, and the government worked to combat it through the public education efforts of the National AIDS Commission under the Ministry of Human Development. NGOs such as the Pan American Social Marketing Organization also actively countered discrimination against persons with HIV/AIDS. The law provides for protection of workers against unfair dismissal, including for HIV status, but no cases have been filed. Studies released during the year showed an increase in perceived discrimination based on HIV status.

Section 7. Worker Rights

a. Freedom of Association and the Right to Collective Bargaining

The law, including related regulations and statutes, generally provides for the right to establish and join trade unions, conduct legal strikes, and bargain collectively. The law also prohibits antiunion discrimination, dissolution, or suspension of unions by administrative authority. The Ministry of Labor recognizes unions and employers associations after they are registered, and the law establishes procedures for the registration and status of trade unions and employers organizations and for collective bargaining.

The law allows authorities to refer disputes involving public and private sector employees who provide "essential services" to compulsory arbitration, prohibit strikes, and terminate actions. The national fire service, postal service, monetary and financial services, civil aviation and airport security services, and port authority pilots and security services are deemed essential services outside of the International Labor Organization definition.

Workers can file complaints with the ministry's Labor Department or seek redress from the courts, although it remained difficult to prove that terminations were due to union activity. The department generally handled labor cases without lengthy delays and dealt with appeals via arbitration outside of the court system. Although the law provides for reinstatement for workers fired for union activity, the courts provided monetary compensation instead.

There was a lack of resources to carry out the mandate of the Department, including a shortage of vehicles and fuel to ensure compliance, particularly in rural areas. There were no complaints of administrative or judicial delays relating to labor complaints and disputes, although in the past labor disputes took an extended time to resolve through the court system. Penalties for violations of association or collective bargaining were not provided.

Freedom of association and the right to collective bargaining were not always respected. Unions operated independently of government and political parties. In January approximately 3,000 teachers and public service workers demonstrated against the government, calling for renewed trade union negotiations to provide salary adjustments. There were no reports of government interference in union activities or of violations related to collective bargaining rights. A union president resigned, however, in the middle of negotiations with the government, citing health and personal reasons. There were no reports that employers refused to bargain, bargained with unions not chosen by workers, or used practices to avoid hiring workers with bargaining rights. Nonetheless, antiunion discrimination and other forms of employer interference in union functions sometimes occurred.

b. Prohibition of Forced or Compulsory Labor

The constitution prohibits all forms of forced or compulsory labor, and the government effectively enforced these provisions in some industries. Penalties for forced or compulsory labor were covered under new antitrafficking laws, which carried sentences of one to 12 years and were comparable to other major offenses. Resources and inspections to deter violations were limited. The government did not provide information on the number of victims removed from forced labor during the year.

Forced labor of both Belizean and foreign women occurred in bars and nightclubs. Migrant men and women were at risk for forced labor in agriculture, fishing, and in the service sector, including restaurants and shops, particularly among the South Asian and Chinese communities. Children also faced forced labor (see section 7.c)

Also see the Department of State's *Trafficking in Persons Report* at www.state.gov/j/tip.

c. Prohibition of Child Labor and Minimum Age for Employment

The law prohibits the employment of children under age 14, although exceptions allow light work for children ages 12 to 13. Persons ages 14 to 18 may be employed only in an occupation that a labor officer has determined is "not injurious to the moral or physical development of nonadults." Children under age 16 are excluded from work in factories, and those under age 18 are excluded from working at night or in certain kinds of employment deemed dangerous. A list of dangerous occupations for young workers had not been adopted as law by the end of the year.

The law permits children to work on family farms and in family-run businesses. National legislation does not address a situation in which child labor is contracted between a parent and the employer. The National Child Labor Policy distinguishes between children engaged in work that is beneficial to their development and those engaged in the worst forms of child labor. The policy identifies children involved in the worst forms of child labor as those engaged in hazardous work, trafficking and child slavery, commercial sexual activities, and illicit activities.

The Department of Labor has primary responsibility for implementing labor policies and enforcing labor laws but had limited dedicated resources to investigate complaints. Inspectors from the Labor and Education Departments are responsible for enforcing these regulations. The penalty for employing a child below minimum age is a fine not exceeding BZ$20 ($10) or imprisonment not exceeding two months. On a second offense, the law stipulates a fine not exceeding BZ$50 ($25) or imprisonment not exceeding four months. There was not enough information provided to determine if the penalties, remediation, and inspections were sufficient to deter violations. There was no information on whether child labor laws were well enforced. There is also a National Child Labor Committee under the National Committee for Families and Children that advocates for policies and legislation to protect children and eliminate child labor. Some children are vulnerable to forced labor, particularly in the agriculture, fishing, and service sectors. Commercial sexual exploitation of children occurred (see section 6, children).

Also see the Department of Labor's *Findings on the Worst Forms of Child Labor* at www.dol.gov/ilab/programs/ocft/tda.htm.

d. Acceptable Conditions of Work

The national minimum wage was BZ$3.30 ($1.65) per hour. A full-time worker receiving the minimum wage earned between one-and-one-half and two times the poverty limit income, depending on the district. The law sets the workweek at no more than six days or 45 hours and requires premium payment for overtime work. Workers are entitled to two working weeks' paid annual holiday. Additionally, there are 13 days designated as public and bank holidays. Employees who work on public and bank holidays are entitled to pay at time-and-a-half except for Good Friday and Christmas, which are paid at twice the normal rate.

Several different health and safety regulations cover numerous industries. The law, which applies to all sectors, prescribes that the employer must take "reasonable care" for the safety of employees in the course of their employment. The law further states that every employer who provides or arranges accommodation for workers to reside at or in the vicinity of a place of employment shall provide and maintain sufficient and hygienic housing accommodations, a sufficient supply of wholesome water, and sufficient and proper sanitary arrangements.

The Ministry of Labor enforced the minimum wage and health and safety regulations to varying degrees. The ministry's Department of Labor had 25 labor officers in 10 offices throughout the country. Inspections were not sufficient to ensure compliance, especially in the more remote areas. Fines varied according to the infraction but generally were not very high. It was unclear whether penalties served as a deterrent. The 2011 Labor Act broadened the definition of unfair dismissal to protect employees and gives broader authority to labor officers to investigate issues of unfair dismissal in addition to earlier powers to ensure employer's compliance with fair compensation. Although several cases were pending, the Labor Tribunal has not convened since it was established.

The minimum wage generally was respected. Nevertheless, anecdotal evidence from NGOs and employers suggested that undocumented Central American workers, particularly young service workers and agricultural laborers, were regularly paid below the minimum wage. Information on workplace fatalities was not available. There were no complaints of major industrial factory fires or mine disasters.

www.ingramcontent.com/pod-product-compliance
Lightning Source LLC
Chambersburg PA
CBHW080810290526
45790CB00008B/3647